P9-DEN-518

ENGLISHMAN'S ROAD

JEREMY HOOKER

ENGLISHMAN'S ROAD

CARCANET NEW PRESS LIMITED

For Sue, Joe and Emily
ac i bobl Llangwyryfon a Threfenter

Acknowledgements and thanks are due to the editors of
publications in which some of these poems first appeared:
The Anglo-Welsh Review, Bananas, Green Horse, Helix
(Australia), *Madog, Other Poetry, Pearl* (Denmark),
Pequod (U.S.A.), *Poems 1976, Poems 1978, PN Review,
Poetry Review, Poetry Wales.* Four of the poems included
in 'A View from the Source' first appeared in the pam-
phlet *The Elements* (1972). Acknowledgements are also
due to H.T.V. and B.B.C. Radio 3 ('Poetry Now').

Copyright © Jeremy Hooker 1980

All Rights Reserved

SBN 85635 322 1

First published in 1980 by
Carcanet New Press Limited
330 Corn Exchange Buildings
Manchester M4 3BG

The Publisher acknowledges the financial assistance of
the Arts Council of Great Britain.

Printed in England by Billings, Guildford.

CONTENTS

PASSAGES

WIND AND SHADOW

1
Day of brief rainbows
and stormy cloud.

Rain drips like dark juice
from blackberries, runs red
from hips and haws.

Where my clogged shoes
take me, wet and happy,
across the fields, under
long, skating shadows,
Hambledon darkens and gleams.

2
Ploughed fields with a scud
of white flint run high,
break at the edge.

Red fruit and yellow leaves,
beeches turning gold,
fall short.
Over the brow I can hear
continual dull thunder.

From my feet,
grass soaked dark as iron,
rounded like a planet,
the hill abruptly starts
its motionless ascent.

3
I let the wind carry me,
half asleep, like a child
who dreams of flying.

It echoes in the cave
of my head, putting out
all but a dim light.

Under my feet
which scarcely touch,
the hill flies up.

4

In the centre of the hill
I crouch.

Brilliant in shivered rays
against black cloud
a cold light falls
but does not settle.
All boundaries are open
to a race of shadows.

Against wind and shadow
the pattern holds,
ring within ring
like a banded shell.

The earth against my back
feels motionless.

In the shelter of the barrow
I rest with eyes still.

Again the rings encircle me.

CROSSING THE NEW BRIDGE (1)

Tongues of mud and shingle
slide away; an Esso tanker
dips towards the Gulf.

Nothing to dwell on there,
or in ground sown
with worked-out bones.

Nor can I be a channel
among the water-ways,
but must cross the new bridge
hiding the Itchen, perhaps

voicing the true relation
in a place of passage.

CROSSING THE NEW BRIDGE (2)

Driving out, with eyes
that never leave the road,
I feel like a slow wader,
dragging foot after lumping foot
from ooze, pulling the tide behind me.

It will cover sticks in the mud;
where I left imaginary prints
waves will spread, with a lick
of scum and a few gulls bobbing.
Now everything will be in place.

CROSSING THE NEW BRIDGE (3)

The clean curve flies over,
without a view.
Below, the old floating-bridge
has wound up its chains for ever.

Driving over, perversely
I walk its decks, watching
the shipping river, the giant tees
of a new bridge being built,
outstretched, not touching.

SARISBURY GREEN

Between pre-war, redbrick houses
comes a sudden break, yachts
admiring their reflections; then
the redbrick church standing
in a dark pool marked with stones.
Here are the bare bones of my people,
nor is there any thing so mean or dull
it does not bring me to the ground,
not even a strip of pavement
by a bus stop. There I enter
the body of a child, impatiently
straining against the arms
that hold him, his arms outstretched
like a swimmer's, reaching out.

AUGUST 1976

Time of long drought—curse
on all greenness: of gorse
burned black where the shore ends,
but tenaciously rooted,
and within, a drying source.

Far out across mud, the pomp
of August rigged,
with spinnakers
of yellow, blue and red;
a sea that seems to float
detached, glacial,
and in near pools, the sun
a buckled hammerhead.

Time to leave: to learn
a way both out and down,
driving away, but feeling
through all that's beaten hard,
a stream that can bear itself.

NEAR WARSASH

River and church remain,
but mainly the names:
these have for me the pattern
of a family album.

But the places have gone,
and where the road now speeds
an almost featureless conjunction,
there is only the cold,
closed face of the south.

Yet there is another rhythm
which I sense driving, being
driven through: the deep channels
of married lives, shelving
inward and bearing on,
under the appearance
of lifeless forms
in a future conurbation,
and houses standing still.

THE COMMON

Furze lives here, between church
and pine copse, on a green
that separates facing houses.
Furze: hard to root out, fuel
of the poor and love evergreen,
whether cowled with snow
or crackling in heat, always
with a few beaked, yellow blooms.
Here cobwebs fly, and any thread
will lead from centre to centre
through a maze of spiky corridors.
Or turn on the roundabout
with children, through a circle
of countless signs.
Here, too, fear is at home,
when threading dark passages
to find all familiars lost.
The bell calls with a dull bong;
furze cut down in the graveyard
grows back, by the marble angel,
graceless, with folded wings.

THE MATERIALS

It was the shapely flints,
the gravels, and every material
underfoot to which I reached out
from the first, coming alive
in wartime to a place of spoilheaps
and pits opened in the ground.

Now it is all closed, and I protest,
grateful for the milk of welfare
in my bones; cry out
against irony's accomodations:
these things have been taken again
without care, and the genius
of deformation unloosed.

Here it broods complacently
on city and suburb, and hopelessness
attends—as if this
were a final settlement.

These materials
in and under the hand
are worth a humane sympathy.

RETURNING

Rain on the road, and a light
in harmony with grainy walls,
with austere wartime dawns
and the grey city smoking.

Here I am sealed out, and pass,
not for the last time:
What is love to be withheld,
asking a return?

UNDER MYNYDD BACH

It must be remembered that the *numina* of the hills see to the metamorphosis of whatever infiltrates those hills.
—David Jones

The fields are greener and the sea bluer because of the unseen company of past generations.
—Ned Thomas, *The Welsh Extremist*

"Nor do I think, that any other nation than this of Wales, or any other language, whatever may hereafter come to pass, shall, in the day of severe examination before the supreme Judge, answer for this corner of the earth."
—Giraldus Cambrensis: the words of the old
Welshman of Pencadair
to Henry II

WINTER PRELUDE

A magpie out of Brueghel
Draws his long, straight tail
Across the cold still-life;
The naked stream runs black
Below the barely parted
Overhangs of snow.
No human voice or chirrup
Where the night fall rests.

A new year, and a snowfall
Hardly marked—still
The unbelieving self is still.
I look from emptiness
Towards the covering snow.

Wales, I find below
Your silence and your sound
A silence harder than the rock
To break and deeper than the snow.

BEIDOG

Sunlight and shallow water,
rock, stones with red marks
like cuts of a rusty axe,
dark under hazel and alder,
broken white on blackened steps
and below the falls a cold pale green—
how shall I celebrate this,
    always present
under our sleep and thoughts,
where we do not see ourselves
    reflected
or know the language of memory
gathered from its fall?

Beidog running dark
    between us
and our neighbours, down
from Mynydd Bach—
this is the stream I wish to praise
    and the small mountain.

I am not of you, tongue
through whom Taliesin descends the ages
gifted with praise, who know
that praise turns dust to light.
    In my tongue,
of all arts
this is the most difficult.

SOFT DAYS AFTER SNOW

Soft days after snow,
    snowdrops
under sycamores beside the stream,
earth brown and crumbling.

Now the dark gleams softly
under catkins and water below,
alight in the February sun.
And I who desired
    eyes washed clean
as melting snow,
radiant at the point of fall,
know that every word obscures
the one I want to know.

Now soft days bear us
who take each other's hands,
and on their surface
    colder than blood
our brief appearances.

Though snowdrops follow the snow,
    and the water burns,
darkness carries them.

Our faces are taken away.

Where do you go,
    unspeakable love?

ON SAINT DAVID'S DAY

For Dewi Sant, an eye
of yellow in the daffodils,
the curlew from the sea,
the hare that lollops by a gate
    which opens wide
on far Plynlimmon,
Cader Idris
and the airy rockface
    of the northern sky.

I too would name
a tribute of these things:
cold wind,
white sun of March,
    the boundaries
whose handywork of stone
shines through the falling earth.

I turn towards the mynydd
in a film of light,
    and turning
ask of Dewi Sant
    his benediction
on these words that settle
where the uplands rise.

APRIL BLIZZARD

The sky closes round me,
narrowing the marsh
to a pool of frogspawn
dappled with snow.

I am caught out
by the thickening swirl,
wading almost blind, somewhere
in the fields gone wild,

till a grey wagtail rises
startled, showing
with a yellow sign
the small stream running back.

DANDELIONS RISE

Now dandelions rise
and the moon goes down
blood-red with fine new horns;
the cuckoo has reached
this edge of the west, and its call
echoes with memories: for this
the grass is not less green
or gorse a cooler gold.
Time is not a dust
that soils their freshness,
but rising like the sap
it makes them burn, and fires
the light with ancient beams
where trees with dead leaves
slipped about their feet now gleam again.

CURLEW

The curve of its cry—
A sculpture
Of the long beak:
A spiral carved from bone.

It is raised
   quickening
From the ground,
Is wound high, and again unwound,
   down
To the stalker nodding
In a marshy field.

It is the welling
Of a cold mineral spring,
Salt from the estuary
Dissolved, sharpening
The fresh vein bubbling on stone.

It is an echo
Repeating an echo
That calls you back.

It looses
Words from dust till the live tongue
Cry: This is mine
Not mine, this life
Welling from springs
Under ground, spiralling
Up the long flight of bone.

THE MASON'S LAW

Though the slate
where his hand slipped
could not stand
    worthy of a name,
at least it could lie
in his living room,
set in the floor.

Er Cof unfinished,
under our feet, recalls
the mason and his law:
    Honour the dead
with your craft;
waste nothing; leave
no botched memorial.

BRYNBEIDOG

For ten years the sycamores
have turned about us, the Beidog
has run with leaves, and ice and sun.
I have turned the earth, thrown up
blue chip and horseshoe; from near fields
sheep and bullocks have looked in.

We have shared weathers
with the stone house; kept its silence;
listened under winds lifting slates
for a child's cry; all we have
the given space has shaped, pointing
our lights seen far off
as a spark among scattered sparks.
    The mountain above
has been rock to my drifting mind.

Where all is familiar, around us
the country with its language
gives all things other names;
there is darkness on bright days
and on the stillest a wind
that will not let us settle,
but blows the dust from loved
things not possessed or known.

WIND BLEW ONCE

Wind blew once till it seemed
the earth would be skinned from the fields,
the hard roots bared.
   Then it was again
a quiet October,
red berries on grey rock
and blue sky, with a buzzard crying.

I scythed half-moons in long grass,
with nettle-burn stinging my arms,
bringing the blood's rhythm back.
   At night
in our room we lay in an angle
between two streams,
with sounds of water meeting,
   and by day
the roads ran farther,
joined and formed a pattern
at the edge of vast, cloudy hills.

   The house was small
against the mountain; from above,
a stone on a steep broad step
of falling fields; but around us
the walls formed a deep channel,
with marks of other lives, holding
its way from worked moorland
to this Autumn with an open sky.

COMMON LAND ABOVE TREFENTER

This is no haunt
For the painter of prospects.

Sheep will not bleat a complaint
Or the barn owl hoot derision,
Where poverty abounded
Providing shelter.

On bared common, where
Nocturnal migrants homed,
There is room for the kite
Cleaned out of cities, none
For the import of terror,

For alien shadow
In common daylight,
Or fashion
Of nightmare or grandeur:

Thin cawl
On the valley's bread line
Is not its provider, nor
Dwellings built in a night,
Fields wide as an axe throw
From the door, patterning
Moorland with stony patches.

Only the bare history
Under foot—holdings

Untenable, falling back
Into quarries: last post
Of hedge-bank craftsmen,
With breast plough and mattock,
On the road to the coalface.

HILL COUNTRY RHYTHMS

for Robert Wells

Sometimes I glimpse a rhythm
I am not part of, and those who are
could never see.
   The hawk I disturb
at his kill, leaving bodiless,
bloody wings spread, curves
away and with a sharp turn
follows the fence; and the fence
lining a rounded bank flies
smoothly downhill, then rises
to wind-bowed trees whose shape
the clouds take on, and the ridge
running under them, where
the sky bears round in a curve.
On the mountainside stands
a square white farm, its roof
a cutting edge, but it too
moves with shadow and cloud.
   I glimpse this
with the hawk in view, lose it
to fenceposts and trees holding
a still day down, and wings
dismembered at my feet, while
down the road comes a neighbour
singing loudly, with his herd
big-uddered, slowly swaying.

AS A THOUSAND YEARS

Not a soul, only
a stubble field, bales
like megaliths; a flight
of trees over the Beidog,
and behind, darker green,
at the back of the sky,
the ridge damming
the sun; then,
    for a breath,
there was no sign of us.
Not a soul, only
light flooding this field,
bright as a marigold.

REVIVAL, 1904

They hung on the word.

It does not matter
the slopes of Hafod Ithel
are empty now; empty
as their farms that summer.

Judgement is the rockface.

It does not matter
you will hear no echo
of prayer or praise
across Llyn Eiddwen's water.

They were crossed with light.

IN A WELSH PRIMARY SCHOOL

for Mari Llwyd

Around me, elements
of this place form a world,
with dragons, flowers,
flying houses on the walls;
shepherds with real crooks
and kings with tinsel crowns.
Here I also come to learn,
and know the same care
Gwion knows, Aled, Ifor
and the rest; and glimpse
through mist between
two languages,
the kindest things of Wales.

Mari, though I stand outside,
may I be numbered still
with all who give you praise.

A NEIGHBOUR

I remembered his laugh—once
he almost fell from a chair;
also with one hammerblow
he drove a fencepost in.
Some weeks I saw only him,
with his dogs and stick, old coat
and greasy cap, walking
from the mountain to his fields;
and we talked—we said aye
to everything, with a language
between us, and rare china
civility, out in wind, rain or sun.
He was first to welcome us,
standing in the door saying aye, aye . . .

I would have seen him then,
strangely white, thinning the hedge
with a hook, his old coat hung on a branch;
but instead a flock of starlings
turned me aside—a swirl
of black flecks over the valley.
Then, seeing the graveyard,
I did not look again
at the hedge, with white, jagged ends.

SHEPHERD

Others have died or left;
he has grown louder, bigger,
filling the fields which he keeps
with an old skill.

I picture him through glass,
framed in the window,
against the mountain:

tall, strongly made,
ruddy from wind and sun,
a man who strides, sings,
waves a stick, then shouts
at his dogs with a voice
they will hear in the village.

And he turns, walks
through the frame, as he has
since he came as a boy
and stood with his father
saying aye, aye . . .

MORRICE PENGELLY

With the stream between us,
a sack on his shoulders,
he stood shouting a welcome.
It was his field, its state
as old as he was; we were
his neighbours, and the field's.

Trenched for a watermain,
cut from end to end,
he watched the incision heal.
Yet it was rough—a world
of many corners; dense
with brambles near the stream;
with mountain ponies on its back,
boulders in long grass, ditches
exposing blue-veined clay.

He is dead now; the stream
runs straight, the field is smooth,
with brown soil finely shaded,
graceful curving lines;
sheepnet and barbed wire fences
on hazel stumps, and where they grew,
keeping its wildness in,
making in late summer a warm
cornucopia of blackberries and nuts,
there is a spacious sky,
a far horizon.
Now it will yield.
It has been joined to the land again.

PWYLL THE OLD GOD

"I would be glad to see a wonder," said Pwyll
"I will go and sit on the hill."

The Mabinogion

Pwyll the old god
may look through you,
when you look through eyes
of spiderwebs, through
tiny rainbows brilliant
as bluebottle shards, and see,
in a dance of gold flecks,
the mountain hang by a strand.

This may be his emblem:
a ram's skull with a thread
of silk between its horns,
but certainly you see
the everyday, the wonder:

Old windblown light
fresh as this morning;
rooks with black breasts
and silver backs; clear-cut
shadows brightening fields,
and over the ridge the sun,
curve of a dark body
in blinding white; everywhere
fragments of web shining,
that look like ends.

EMILY

The season is late; our long shadow
with two clothes peg heads notched
one above the other lies flat across the field;
and from above me, breaking
the quiet of sleepy baas and caws,
an excited voice exclaims
at a sudden vision:
    a yellow digger
uprooting bushes, changing the stream's
meanders to a straighter course.

Now our single track divides,
a dark fork in dew-grey grass,
and a small girl in a red frock,
sun yellowing her fair hair, runs
away from me with a bunch
of corn marigolds, campion,
harebells and a magpie feather
crushed in her fist.

Away she runs through a drift
of thistledown, seeds
stuck to her bare wet legs;
runs away laughing, shouting
for me to catch her—
but I know now that I never will;
    never, my darling;
but run with care, run lightly
with the light about you,
run to the gate through moist soft grass,
webs and bright blades all about you,
    hint of a rainbow
in the silver shower at your heels.

LINES TO A BROTHER

To Tony Hooker

Waking early today,
I think of you preparing
for work, driving through
a quiet Oxfordshire dawn.

    You will join
sawn timbers, intimate
as their owners will never be
with roof-tree and joist,
while I lie awake, watching
light form the bulk of Mynydd Bach.

    I see your hands,
steadied by the recreation
of labour, and again
the morning air tastes thin;
    once more I turn
to images of the skilled life
we have drawn from and shared,
in whose absence
my words offer no habitation.

BEHIND THE LIGHTS

Last night, I looked from the Island.
    Then I was again
behind the lights, living there
blindly, where the mainland
long shore shone, with breaks
at Forest and river mouths,
a ghostly smoke round chimneys;
till suddenly, a green light
on black water cut across my view.

Tonight, I return
to another darkness, the house
strangely cold; behind me
the long road back to Wales.
It will be dark in an hour
but now the sun setting
picks out a fox in the field
above the house, cutting across my view.
There he goes gingerly,
a lordly fox, golden red.
    Tired, I see
a green light on black water.
Better to follow the fox,
from sunlight into shadow,
on his cold way home.

EXILE'S COUNTRY

for Ned Thomas

1

On streets far from here,
their eyes are suddenly vacant.

They follow lanes of rowans
to the ridge, and share
the buzzard's sky.

Another spirit comes
on a day that began with frost,
when a red admiral pauses
on a sun-warmed trunk,
briefly transfixed.

They haunt the hearths
of stonecropped ruins,
colder for their unseen hands,
and come to look again
from blind Blaenbeidog
and Nantcwtta with its owl;
or launch a ghostly boat
from Eiddwen's
half-stopped harbour mouth.

2

At evening we shiver,
when a tree catches light;
and before dawn, hearing
the wind rise from silence.

Tufts of sheep's wool
on a barbed wire fence
may also be their sign,
and ravens playing dead,
that tumble from the sky.

They also colour
every smallest thing,
from rowans red as glowing coal
to sea and mountains in the north.

They also bring
the pain of love
that's bodiless and cannot stay.

WINTER THRUSHES

From Cardigan to Llŷn,
Off clear grey sea, the clean wind
Bares the darker mountains
Of the north, and where I walk,
Draws freezing tears and drives
The winter thrushes to the haws.

But these before my eyes
Are vague; their flight restores
A frozen redwing to my hand, and
Fieldfares to New Forest fields.
Then how may I be present here,
And tell my wishes from the truth?

46

PRAYER IN JANUARY

Now when the old New Year
Starts red with sun on snow,
Must resolution splinter
Like a frosted bough?
The stars of ancient January
Hurt the eyes; by day, like stars,
Snow crystals make them ache.
But Yahweh's eyes burn clear
As drops that fall from alders
By the mountain stream.
They are not stars or melting snow
But outstare every star
And every thing most star-like
In this old, cold, flaming universe.

Soft heart, small, bitter pool
Beneath your darkening hemisphere
Of ice, hidden eyes blaze
Where you hide. Regard
Their hard regard, that weighs
The worth of all you guard
At not a fraction of its price.
Let love outlast such love
As self, too tender of itself,
Has dreamed regardless of a sight
More pitiless, more pitiful than you.
Then be unselved, or drying
When the eyes burn through
Die dreamless into hard-ribbed clay.

SYCAMORE BUDS

Then speak, not
from the shell of self,
its beaten walls, but
as these pointed buds
with tight, green scales
the winter could not loose
and waste the rising force
erecting spikes, that
lengthen, curving
into soft, closed beaks
that open on their tongues
and now unfold small hands:
wrinkled, blood-red leaves,
fresh and glistening
damp—shapes of the force
they are, containing them.

DRAGONS IN THE SNOW

Thaw to the hedgerows
left white crosses on the hill;
   the first thrush sang.

Now a buzzard cries, confirming
   silence under all.

The few bare trees are darker
for the fall that covers
   boundaries,
and in their place reveals
contrasting absolutes.

We are so small,
the boy and I, between
the snowclouds and the snow.

He starts from here,
who talks of dragons
as we walk, the first today
to leave a human sign
beside the marks of sheep and crow

He warms me
with confiding hand
and fiery talk,
   who also start
upon the ground
of choice, the silence
answering the choice;
happy to be small, and walk,
and hear of dragons in the snow.

A VIEW FROM THE SOURCE (1968-1973)

TO A WELSH POET

1
Death
Stiffens
The green limb.

The power men make
Makes them powerless,
For a time:
A charred corpse
Burnt in the steelworks,
Is a furnace of anger,
Resistance, pain.

2
A small man, around
Him the granite walls
Of Dartmoor.
His jailors face away
Listening for gunfire
In a corner of Europe.
And he is sustained,
On this front,
By the secret passages
Of speech.

Not one man, but many,
Living and dead,
Stiffening
In corrupted ground.

3
He was on the far side
Of another language,
An old man I never spoke to,
In the next room.

Five years later,
Facing deep into England
I could ask him:

Teach me now,
To speak to the living.

JET OVER MYNYDD BACH

Before I see him he is miles away,
Below me, trailing thunder.
And I might be where giants
Hurled stone javelins from cantred into cantred
And left a pile of mountains where they shook
The pebbles from their boots.

The long grass knows one kind of time,
That makes a graveyard of abandoned
Settlements, green mound of drystone wall,
Humps where buildings were;
The time another year's tormentil serves
With yellow stars; of brambles, and the hill itself
Across the bay from Llŷn
With Bardsey's barrow at the tip:
Peninsula now floating in another world,
Now inundated by a tide of mist,
Unchangeing only to the inconceivable.

I wonder what he sees,
Connected to us by a chain of politics,
Potential sunburst and a startled curse,
My half-admiring eye that, as I watch,
Is left unfocused on the empty blue,
Returning giddy in an instant to the walls,
The stairway mounting straight into the sky.

LANDSCAPE

1 *Rock and Fern*

Inches away a beck slices the hill.
Catching my breath, I rest under the last thorn.
After it there's nothing green,
Only smooth stones, russet scrub,
And among the whin, rough stones.
But here, on a rock blanched by it,
The sun prints the shadow of a fern,
Still as a fossil, pointed like a arrowhead:
The mottoed tablet to an aeon.
A breeze jigs the fern,
And between moments of perfect white
The rock flickers. Then the wind stops
And the fern stiffens, a shadow bedded in rock.
Feeling invisible, I climb on.

2 *Rock and Water*

The beck strikes down,
Jabbing wittily through narrows,
Stopping to consider a slow pool
And sliding out cleanly over domes of rock.
At a bend the air decays,
Rotting for yards beyond the carcass,
Bone needles stuck through a mess of wool.

Bleached pates of rock, shreds of foam
Dull beside quartz, the sunstone glittering.
At intervals, unscoured rock piles
Keep a quiet like sacked monasteries.
And everything's hot to touch.
My shadow moons in a pool
Or lies crooked and breaking in shallows;
Delicately, a trout flicks through its head.

3 *At the Source*

Sheep jump up around me,
Their long skulls chock with horror.
The hills have heard little but bleating
Since the glaciers went by.

But I forget the pipit
Startled by my drudging boots, wrenching the eye
Upwards, the gaze beaten back
But for an instant free of spaces
Where a separate music's made.
I forget many things, mainly things:
The multiple unreckoned differences.
In the heat my hands swell and fluch
Tightening the ring on my finger.

At the source
The mean bitten grass becomes mush
Reddish-brown, with islands of moss.
But I cannot call it the source.
The beck's been fed all the way
By others of equal size.
This one's no bigger than a puddle:
A small clear pool with a hint of iron.
I breathe over it, earthbound and aching.

The hills bleat.
The pipits address miles of air.

4 *A View from the Source*

The century drew out
Freighted with ore, jolting upline,
To stake with a bayonet acres of dead.

It had served; it could fail,
Poison the beck, and the beck

Empty its puffed white fish on the sea;
The place gutted, forgotten.

I can imagine the dark dispelled
By prosperous light; miners break earth;
All that's impossible
But ghosts in a place so dead.
A stone pitched in the shaft
Plummets from hearing with a metallic ring.

CARRYING HAY

for Dafydd ap Griffith

We pass a tin cup
For the gulp
Of water, the splash
On a red back
Gummed with straw,
And through fingers
Easing the joints
Bitten by string.

Trees in shadow ripen
Like plums out of reach
And the bales swung
From hand to hand
Get heavier, building
The last steep load
On the trailer, until,
Senses half-asleep,
We sway from the bare field,
Each slack link dreaming.

PEMBROKESHIRE JOURNEY

for Peter Clarke

I *Encounter at Pentre Ifan*

It looks weird from the road,
Like a monstrous spider crab.

Approaching through a narrow
Earth-banked path, we emerge
To a broader sky.

Stone-walled fields shelve
Mistily towards the sea,
Under the ghost of a clouded sun.

Here it is congruous:
Stone in a field of stones;
But still exotic,
With the unnatural grace
Of man.

The capstone balances
On uprights like a boat
Inverted for the winter.

It is spacious under the roof,
In the house of the dead.

Others approach; you greet them
Familiarly, with surprise.
We stand shadowed.

Inevitable that we should say,
'Wales is a small country.'

II *At Nevern*

1

Near a mounting block
Where children swing their legs
We park the car, and enter

A dark passage under yews.
Here a tree bleeds, with gashed,
Viscous side, and beyond it

The Celtic cross still stands
Taller than two men, a bald
Roundhead monolith wrought

With swastika and maze.
There are many entrances.
Which one shall we take?

2

Here the Irish Sea blew in
A half-savage culture—
Of gold, manuscripts, slaves.

Maglocunus was the first,
His stone notched in ogham.

Perhaps we come only
For the name, or because
A green streak makes us haunt it,
Like lichen on the walls.

3

Whether true or false
No one here can tell.

Nothing limits fancy
In a place of dead
We did not care for.

For the tombstone poet
It was different.
His yards of doggerel
Meant more to someone
Than Shakespeare or ap Gwilym.

Here beneath this flowery sod
Lies our rosebud, withered, dead.

We are curious and cannot
Care enough even for the graves
Of children not our own.

For us, the only entrance
Leads away.

III *Walking the Cliff Path*

   1
As we climb, head and lungs clear,
The sky lifts, the blue-grey sea
Reflects a watery sun.

From cliffs with gulls below
The eye falls south, over
Arched, long-necked
Headlands, and returns
In a slow flight inland
From islands of volcanic rock.

Then the path descends
Into a hollow of gorse
And stonechats; heat brings out
The flies that love us; we clump
With skewed feet over stones.

   2
At Carregwastad Point
We rest.

The 'last invasion'
Ended here, in drunkenness
And pillage.

Why here? Pen Caer
Was its own protector.
Still only the sea wastes it,
And the acid lichen.

If I could paint
I would use its colours
On a surface of stone.

Blue-grey for the sea.
Green and brown earth colours.
Yellow for tormentil.
Red for the brick defences
Of a later war.

For the billy goat
That lives there,
Wagging his beard,
The colour of rock itself.

3

Some stones I return to
For those they commemorate;
To others for themselves.

We cannot read this one
To Dewi Emrys.

Your Welsh soon falters.
I stand monoglot before it.

And because we cannot read it,
We turn aside, listening
To a yellowhammer repeating
Its dry whistle on a thorn.

It is like a bird practising
To sing; but this is its song,
Ending always with a *Tzee*.

IV *Sleeping out on Pen Caer*

We are not mystics
Though this was their country:
Crested headlands
Like stone dragons drinking,

Haunt of hermit and guillemot;
Swirl of white islands
Where the current bore them,
Crucifix for pilot, among the seals.

We could have had a warm bed,
But chose discomfort, cold,
Feeling the earth
With our bones, under
The immense pale drifts of the Milky Way.

We have our whisky and tobacco.
We belong as much to jets
That pass above, as to the stars.

Before light the gulls' cries
Wake an older earth; hoarse and shrill,
The salt cry of rocky islands.

The sun appears, a red ball
Over the volcanic crags
Of Garn Fawr.

Out at sea the esses of a breeze
Lie like the marks of a lash
Flicked on a smooth insensible hide.

ENGLISHMAN'S ROAD

ENGLISHMAN'S ROAD

for Peter Lord

First Voice
> Ruins among the rushes, stairs
> mounting straight into the sky.
> Walls that shelter sheep
> from the west wind, or turn
> like drystone streams, back
> to their quarry source.
> What is here but death?

Second Voice
> Watch for the early settlers.
> For the chamber-builders in stone,
> who made a house for the dead.
> For the shell-borne saint,
> the houseless one, for whom
> the universe is home.
> Watch for an Irish or a Viking sail.
> Watch for the castle-builders.
> For incomers, early and late,
> on the Englishman's road.

First Voice
> What did they settle for,
> the nightbuilders?
> And why did he come,
> the young man from Lincolnshire?
> I should know why he came,
> who also settle, and ask
> with an English tongue:
> what can I make of this
> long-settled ground?

Second Voice
> Take a long view from Mynydd Bach: let your eye rise
> and fall with ridges that stone walls or bent thorns
> follow—green dragon backs, crested like petrified break-
> ers; yet also the walls are always climbing or in flight.

This is a country of vast spaces: it rolls with hidden hollows to the mountains of the north, against the sweep of sea—

> preternatural grey,
> the mountains of Llŷn
> a chain of islands,
> or blue as spirit flame,
> or a lunula of beaten gold.

Here the buzzard with broad wings spread draws a widening circle, ringing an intricate pattern of commons and enclosures, whitewashed farms and red-roofed barns.

At night an irregular pattern of lights reflects the stars.

Here the western light is always changing, too quick for the eye though it notes

> grey mystery
> of April, haunted
> by the curlew's salty cry,
> or August
> floating the hills,
> or Winter
> with a hard whiteness
> hammering the ground.

And what the light changes is only a face—face of a work vaster and more laboured than the pyramids; but continuing. For this is settled country, its pattern absorbent, deeply ingrained, but unfinished; without the finality of a coiled fossil, though it too is a life wrought in rock. And here these English words play on a surface through which they cannot shine, to illumine its heart; they can possess the essence of this place no more than the narrow road under the Welsh mountain can translate its name.

> Lon Sais it is called,
> not Englishman's Road.

Two hundred years ago
      the first nightbuilders came
and on these commons they built,
      invoking an ancient but unwritten right.
Then it was said:

Squatter
There shall not be any large farms or houses built on
Mynydd Bach but they shall be pulled down, but if any
poor man shall come, then we shall build a house and
make a field and help him.

First Voice
Ruins among the rushes, stairs
mounting straight into the sky.
This too was the place of a skull.

Second Voice
Watch their craft by lanternlight.
It is late October. Now the night is not too short; strong
winds and heavy rains are still to come. Their materials
are all to hand. They have loaded on carts—

        stone
        timber
        clods
        soil
        turf

Theirs is the hedge-bank craft. They pack the walls
together with napes of mattocks. Turves cut from the
moorland with a breast-plough cover the rafters; open
coils of sheaves laid on the roof are fastened in place
with reeds. The thatch covers from apex to eaves.

And now it is grey light, before the sun climbs on this
mountain, as it seems to farmers on the richer lowlands,
preparing to milk; and now with the first smoke, a soft

plume on the roof, a man with a good arm takes his
axe, and from the doorway hurls it. Where it falls he
draws a line, rounding his portion of thin grass with
rocky shoals.

It is settled. The long struggle with famine begins.

First Voice
    Kite country. On the moorland
    a car's wheelless corroding shell.
    Slopes pitted with Iron Age graves
    like stopped wells, and here,
    green lanes leading—where?
    Not a door to knock on; within
    all's spiritless, a draughty space.
    Ruins among rushes, stairs
    mounting straight into the sky.
    Walls that shelter sheep
    from the west wind, or turn
    like drystone streams, back
    to their quarry source.
    What can I make of this?
    Emptiness. The exquisite, cruel
    colours of decay. Death's absolute.

Squatter
    Aye, it was dark, it was damp,
    But we came homeless, and this
    We held, for a time.
    A huddle of hovels
    If you like, and always
    With enemies—
    Where all's common it must be so—
    Boyos from down below,
    Fat-earth men, after their peat
    And turf and grazing;
    But worst, the weather, and this
    Rockbacked, lock-jawed land.

But that man, that
Young sir, him we served, him
We gave what he could make
Of us. We half-roasted him.
And if at last we lost,
Still I tell you, this was no dream.
This was the Promised Land.
We were Bethel folk. We built
Stone on stone, a house of praise.
And what did He promise
But toil, sweat of the brow,
Bitter bread? So we laboured
And the spirit moved us, light
To the leaden hills, a feast
To the starving frame; laboured
I tell you, and praised, not
For honeyed ease, but at the last
Peace and an eternal rest.

Second Voice
And to this place, into this pattern,
      in the Spring of 1820, came
a small, dark Englishman
      from a Hall in Lincolnshire.

It was not then Lon Sais
      where he rode on horseback,
curlews crying in the marshy fields,
      cuckoo calling back to cuckoo
until the mountain sounded hollow
      echoing their name.

Now the common land was his,
      for two guineas an acre,
but still it remained to settle:
      by building a house with a prospect,
      by improvement.

He called himself:
                    Augustus Brackenbury,
                    gentleman
                    of the town of Aberystwyth
                    in the county of Cardigan.

And the people of Mynydd Bach called him:

                    Sais Bach.

It was not then Lon Sais,
        but truly, for a time,
the Englishman's road.
     .   .   .

First Voice
    Sais Bach, little Englishman:
    why did he come?
    Must I answer for him,
    who make a shape of the place?

    Which wilderness
    does not know our image?
    Where there is land and sea,
    riches to claim,
    a people without God, or with Him,
    or gods of their own:
    there is our image, and there
    our rootless rongue.

        The stars
    reflect our fires; we are mirrored
    in histories we did not write.

        And here,
    close to home, we have come
    sword against sword, tongue
    against tongue; and by our way
    the people leave, and we pass them,
        as if into our own.

Second Voice
And what the stranger comes to is darkness—not ess-
entially dark, but rather a light he cannot see by. For
he brings with him a mist, which is not the mist of these
hills which bears them away yet is part of them, and in
its clear drops globes their world; but the mist that
swirls from his mouth and clouds his eyes.

Behind the landscape he sees
        there is another.
He cannot hint at
        mountains and fields unseen,
deep and distinct in their native light.

These are measured heights. They are mapped and
named; but still, from without, essentially unknown.
For here these English words play on a surface through
which they cannot shine.

First Voice
I should know why he came,
who also settle, and ask
with an English tongue:
what can I make of this
long-settled ground?

Augustus Brackenbury
Here was a track like a dry river-bed
with cart ruts and stones.
So it had been all the way uphill
from Aberystwyth—where in all that country
I found tolerable company.
All around me was mountain wilderness,
with hovels on my ground
and dark, unsmiling faces. To these
I addressed myself kindly,
but in silence they stared back,
understanding not a word. Yet

this was a day when the sun shone
and cuckoos and curlews called
as if to greet me. And what I saw
was not a hostile wilderness
but a gentleman's seat, a fair prospect,
my estate, my establishment.
There, as in a landscape
of the English school, I saw
wild nature subdued to parkland
and the people graced with benevolence.
Here I would plant myself, and like
a spreading oak shelter my dependents.

Second Voice
   How could he know where he was,
       or that on that mountain,
  where he held himself proudly, he was
       a small, black speck crawling,
  caught in the weave of a pattern
       into which he had blindly come?

  How could he know where he was?
       Or others before and after him?
  incomers, early and late,
       on the Englishman's road.
  Castle-builders, makers
       with words or stone.

  The ruins are taken back.
       From north to south,
  the country echoes their names.

  In the year of Waterloo
       enclosure surveyors came.
  The women showed them a pit.
       Next time, they said,
  bring a sack for your bones.

First Voice
    Habitations of wretchedness,
            generality of the suffering poor.

Squatter
    That was their truth, not ours,
    Not the whole of it.
    We were hungry for land;
    Our thin grass kept a thin flesh
    Firm: peat for our fires, oats,
    A few sheep; for the rest,
    Harvesting of corn and potatoes
    In the seasons, or crawling
    The narrow seams of Ystwyth,
    Under the leaden hills.
    But with spirit for that, so
    Our common rights held, so
    In smoke-filled darkness
    Grace lit our spirit flame.
    I tell you, this was no dream.

Augustus Brackenbury
    I saw a promise in that land:
    of Hafod and Thomas Johnes,
    of a seat gracing the wilderness.
    I saw a park watered by streams
    of Mynydd Bach, prosperity
    for all, a gentle culture, and a civil tongue.

Squatter
    But that man, in his face
    We saw a dream, his dream,
    Ourselves its material.
    Graciously he spoke,
    A gentleman of fashion, or
    After their fashion,
    A gentleman. But I ask you,
    What makes a man? Aye,
    And what did he say?

Few understood, but I knew
His tongue and its meaning:
This is my country: be
Honoured that I come for you
To serve me, and improve you.
And what did we say?

There shall not be any large farms or houses built on
Mynydd Bach but they shall be pulled down.

Second Voice
There is law, and there are rights.
Those who claim rights need a strong hand to hold
them.

Guineas may buy a man the law, but if he is far from his
kind, if between him and the law there comes an invis-
ible but immovable body, of language and loyalty, then
he too may hold his own, and pay for strong hands to
grasp it.

Then the struggle is hand to hand.

Squatter
Was not John Jones son
Of David Jones shamefully
Abused, his horse and cart
Plunged in a bog?
Joshua Davies also—his cart
They broke, and stole his turf.
And Elizabeth Jones,
Going from service on a visit
To her parents, did not Brackenbury
And one of his bullies drag her,
With imprecations, to a deep moat
Surrounding his castle? Aye
And would have thrown her in,
Only one who heard her cries
Ran to help—and was threatened

With a musket to his head,
His lip gashed with a blow
From the muzzle. This was so,
I tell you: these things
In a manner most barbarous
Have been done. And other
Atrocities (too numerous
To mention), no person passing
But insulted, assaulted,
Pursued and shot at.
This on the Sabbath too,
By bullies with fire arms,
Shovels and other implements
Fit for evil purposes.
What justice for us? None.
But I tell you, such cruelties
We will not endure.

Second Voice
    Now again there are lights on the mountain,
            not lanterns but torchflames:
    in their ruddy glow, a slow dance—
            shadowy figures
    treading with measured deliberation.

    They are shawled, they look like women;
    but some are men's faces the lights shine on.

    Brands colour them a deep blood-red. They might have
    risen from the Iron Age graves, here to enact an antique
    ritual, treading the measure of an ancient law.

Augustus Brackenbury
    My estate is situated in the midst of the most desp-
    erate characters, who commit all kind of depredations
    with impunity. The encroachers are so numerous and so
    lawless, that they aid and assist each other to enclose
    the waste lands and to keep possession thereof. This

country is now labouring under a dreadful and deplorable want of morality.

Second Voice
It is rights they come for. There are:

> Jack Rhos goch
> Tom Ffospompren
> David Jones Lledrod
> Jack y Crydd

and others with a good arm to hurl a brand.

They have lit a fire on the mountain.

They circle in a shadowy outer darkness beyond the flames. They have vanished.

Augustus Brackenbury
I have found the peasantry of this part deceitful, treacherous and false swearers. This definition of their national character is agreeable to the general opinion now entertained of them.
Because I am an Englishman I am never to impeach or discover any one who should commit any outrage on the property I possess.

Second Voice
Now the flames show what they consume: a house, burning. An empty house, for there through the darkness go Brackenbury and his bodyguard, shivering, weaponless.

He is almost used to this. Though this is the first firing, twice before he has built, and twice the pickaxe has unhoused him.

Now a lowland farmer, looking up, might think a red moon was rising, with burning horns; but there are few who do not know, and few who have not sworn.

First Voice
> They have vanished; they have made
> their marks on the mountain's face,
> which does not regard them;
> where the kite may prey
> undisturbed, and cloud shadows
> seem the only spirits.
> What is here, in a place
> of sheep and ruins,
> with no door to knock on,
> under a vast empty sky
> which the noise of war planes fills?

Second Voice
> Watch for the early settlers.
> For the chamber-builders in stone,
> who made a house for the dead.
> For the shell-borne saint,
> the houseless one, for whom
> the universe is home.
> Watch for an Irish or a Viking sail.
> Watch for the nightbuilders.
> For incomers, early and late.

First Voice
> Ruins among the rushes, stairs
> mounting straight into the sky.
> Walls that shelter sheep
> from the west wind, or turn
> like drystone streams, back
> to their quarry source.
> This too was the place of a skull.
> What is here but death?

Second Voice
> The nightbuilders have gone—
> > South, over the mountain,
> to coalface and furnace;
> > others were absorbed here,

to coalface and furnace;
    others were absorbed here,
their hovels taken in by stronger walls.
    Original floor and hearth stones
form a pattern with the new—
    all from the mountain.

First Voice
    I will not make them a song;
        they have their songs.
    Nor will I make them an elegy.
        In this pattern they live:
    ridges with walls climbing or in flight,
        hedgebanks squaring the fields,
    in all the work wrought in rock
        they show their hands,
    and there in Bethel,
            flame of spirit
            house of praise.

    Where
        if not in the place of a skull
          will we find
            a vision of the Promised Land?

Second Voice
    This is Lon Sais. Augustus Brackenbury, gentleman, has taken the road to Marylebone. There in 1874 he and his memories will die. But here the memory of Sais Bach will haunt the houseless commons of Mynydd Bach.

Augustus Brackenbury
    I was a pioneer.
    I would improve the waste.
    But these people I could make
    nothing of.
            I would be
   a tree planted by the rivers

of water, that bringeth forth
fruit in his season.
They answered: *the ungodly*
are not so: but are like
the chaff which the wind
drivether away.

Hiraeth, they say,
hiraeth, as if only they
know longing. Lord,
what days I have seen,
buried alive, looking east
with the eyes of my heart!
O to have been a seed
on the west wind, borne
back to Lincolnshire,
if only to grass a grave!
Still I stayed, for a time.
The right was mine, the law
no Welshman would enforce,
because I was English. . .

Second Voice
These are measured heights: a practice run for war
planes. Here curlews come in March, and on a telegraph
pole, with wires running east and west, a buzzard settles,
like a carved figurehead. This is Lon Sais, under the
mountain.

There are ruins among rushes in the near fields. The
castle of Sais Bach is a square ditch, with only moor
grass to impede the wind.

There are no lights on the mountains, unless the moon,
or the beams of a car, driving north through miles of
darkness. There, where carts loaded with turf descended.

This is settled country, an intricate pattern of farms and smallholdings, with Bethel in a hollow. A work wrought in rock, vaster and more laboured than the pyramids; but unfinished. And here these English words play on a surface through which they cannot shine, to illumine its heart; they can possess the essence of this place no more than the narrow road under the Welsh mountain can translate its name.

The place Augustus Brackenbury could not possess
    Sais Bach has entered:
        memory calls back to memory
          echoing his name.

Lon Sais goes on.
Englishman's Road has ended.